# THIS PLAN BOOK BELONGS TO:

_____

## GRADE LEVEL: _____

## SCHOOL YEAR: _____

# WEEK AT A *Glance*

| | MONDAY | TUESDAY | WEDNESDAY | THURSDAY | FRIDAY |
|---|---|---|---|---|---|
| GROUP: | | | | | |
| GROUP: | | | | | |
| GROUP: | | | | | |
| GROUP: | | | | | |
| GROUP: | | | | | |

# WEEK AT A *Glance*

| | MONDAY | TUESDAY | WEDNESDAY | THURSDAY | FRIDAY |
|---|---|---|---|---|---|
| GROUP: | | | | | |
| GROUP: | | | | | |
| GROUP: | | | | | |
| GROUP: | | | | | |
| GROUP: | | | | | |

# WEEK AT A *Glance*

| | MONDAY | TUESDAY | WEDNESDAY | THURSDAY | FRIDAY |
|---|---|---|---|---|---|
| GROUP: | | | | | |
| GROUP: | | | | | |
| GROUP: | | | | | |
| GROUP: | | | | | |
| GROUP: | | | | | |

# WEEK AT A *Glance*

|  | MONDAY | TUESDAY | WEDNESDAY | THURSDAY | FRIDAY |
|---|---|---|---|---|---|
| GROUP: |  |  |  |  |  |
| GROUP: |  |  |  |  |  |
| GROUP: |  |  |  |  |  |
| GROUP: |  |  |  |  |  |
| GROUP: |  |  |  |  |  |

# WEEK AT A *Glance*

| | MONDAY | TUESDAY | WEDNESDAY | THURSDAY | FRIDAY |
|---|---|---|---|---|---|
| GROUP: | | | | | |
| GROUP: | | | | | |
| GROUP: | | | | | |
| GROUP: | | | | | |
| GROUP: | | | | | |

# WEEK AT A *Glance*

| | MONDAY | TUESDAY | WEDNESDAY | THURSDAY | FRIDAY |
|---|---|---|---|---|---|
| GROUP: | | | | | |
| GROUP: | | | | | |
| GROUP: | | | | | |
| GROUP: | | | | | |
| GROUP: | | | | | |

# WEEK AT A *Glance*

| | MONDAY | TUESDAY | WEDNESDAY | THURSDAY | FRIDAY |
|---|---|---|---|---|---|
| GROUP: | | | | | |
| GROUP: | | | | | |
| GROUP: | | | | | |
| GROUP: | | | | | |
| GROUP: | | | | | |

# WEEK AT A *Glance*

| | MONDAY | TUESDAY | WEDNESDAY | THURSDAY | FRIDAY |
|---|---|---|---|---|---|
| GROUP: | | | | | |
| GROUP: | | | | | |
| GROUP: | | | | | |
| GROUP: | | | | | |
| GROUP: | | | | | |

# WEEK AT A *Glance*

|  | MONDAY | TUESDAY | WEDNESDAY | THURSDAY | FRIDAY |
|---|---|---|---|---|---|
| GROUP: |  |  |  |  |  |
| GROUP: |  |  |  |  |  |
| GROUP: |  |  |  |  |  |
| GROUP: |  |  |  |  |  |
| GROUP: |  |  |  |  |  |

# WEEK AT A *Glance*

| | MONDAY | TUESDAY | WEDNESDAY | THURSDAY | FRIDAY |
|---|---|---|---|---|---|
| GROUP: | | | | | |
| GROUP: | | | | | |
| GROUP: | | | | | |
| GROUP: | | | | | |
| GROUP: | | | | | |

# WEEK AT A *Glance*

| | MONDAY | TUESDAY | WEDNESDAY | THURSDAY | FRIDAY |
|---|---|---|---|---|---|
| GROUP: | | | | | |
| GROUP: | | | | | |
| GROUP: | | | | | |
| GROUP: | | | | | |
| GROUP: | | | | | |

# WEEK AT A *Glance*

| | MONDAY | TUESDAY | WEDNESDAY | THURSDAY | FRIDAY |
|---|---|---|---|---|---|
| GROUP: | | | | | |
| GROUP: | | | | | |
| GROUP: | | | | | |
| GROUP: | | | | | |
| GROUP: | | | | | |

# WEEK AT A *Glance*

| | MONDAY | TUESDAY | WEDNESDAY | THURSDAY | FRIDAY |
|---|---|---|---|---|---|
| GROUP: | | | | | |
| GROUP: | | | | | |
| GROUP: | | | | | |
| GROUP: | | | | | |
| GROUP: | | | | | |

# WEEK AT A *Glance*

| | MONDAY | TUESDAY | WEDNESDAY | THURSDAY | FRIDAY |
|---|---|---|---|---|---|
| GROUP: | | | | | |
| GROUP: | | | | | |
| GROUP: | | | | | |
| GROUP: | | | | | |
| GROUP: | | | | | |

# WEEK AT A *Glance*

| | MONDAY | TUESDAY | WEDNESDAY | THURSDAY | FRIDAY |
|---|---|---|---|---|---|
| GROUP: | | | | | |
| GROUP: | | | | | |
| GROUP: | | | | | |
| GROUP: | | | | | |
| GROUP: | | | | | |

# WEEK AT A *Glance*

| | MONDAY | TUESDAY | WEDNESDAY | THURSDAY | FRIDAY |
|---|---|---|---|---|---|
| GROUP: | | | | | |
| GROUP: | | | | | |
| GROUP: | | | | | |
| GROUP: | | | | | |
| GROUP: | | | | | |

# WEEK AT A *Glance*

| | MONDAY | TUESDAY | WEDNESDAY | THURSDAY | FRIDAY |
|---|---|---|---|---|---|
| GROUP: | | | | | |
| GROUP: | | | | | |
| GROUP: | | | | | |
| GROUP: | | | | | |
| GROUP: | | | | | |

# LESSON *Plan*

GROUP:                                          DATE:

BOOK TITLE:                             LEVEL:

## TEACHING POINT / STRATEGY

| WORD WORK | VOCABULARY |
|---|---|
| | |

## BEFORE READING

## DURING READING

## AFTER READING

## NOTES

# ANECDOTAL Notes

| STUDENT NAME | OBSERVATIONS | NOTES |
|---|---|---|
|  |  |  |
|  |  |  |
|  |  |  |
|  |  |  |
|  |  |  |
|  |  |  |

# LESSON *Plan*

| GROUP: | DATE: |
|---|---|
| BOOK TITLE: | LEVEL: |

## TEACHING POINT / STRATEGY

| WORD WORK | VOCABULARY |
|---|---|
| | |

### BEFORE READING

### DURING READING

### AFTER READING

### NOTES

# ANECDOTAL *Notes*

| STUDENT NAME | OBSERVATIONS | NOTES |
|---|---|---|
|  |  |  |
|  |  |  |
|  |  |  |
|  |  |  |
|  |  |  |
|  |  |  |

# LESSON *Plan*

GROUP:                                 DATE:

BOOK TITLE:                         LEVEL:

## TEACHING POINT / STRATEGY

| WORD WORK | VOCABULARY |
| --- | --- |
| | |

## BEFORE READING

## DURING READING

## AFTER READING

## NOTES

# ANECDOTAL *Notes*

| STUDENT NAME | OBSERVATIONS | NOTES |
|---|---|---|
| | | |
| | | |
| | | |
| | | |
| | | |
| | | |

# LESSON *Plan*

| | |
|---|---|
| GROUP: | DATE: |
| BOOK TITLE: | LEVEL: |

## TEACHING POINT / STRATEGY

| WORD WORK | VOCABULARY |
|---|---|
| | |

## BEFORE READING

## DURING READING

## AFTER READING

## NOTES

# ANECDOTAL *Notes*

| STUDENT NAME | OBSERVATIONS | NOTES |
|---|---|---|
|  |  |  |
|  |  |  |
|  |  |  |
|  |  |  |
|  |  |  |
|  |  |  |

# LESSON *Plan*

| GROUP: | DATE: |
|---|---|
| BOOK TITLE: | LEVEL: |

### TEACHING POINT / STRATEGY

| WORD WORK | VOCABULARY |
|---|---|
| | |

### BEFORE READING

### DURING READING

### AFTER READING

### NOTES

# ANECDOTAL *Notes*

| STUDENT NAME | OBSERVATIONS | NOTES |
|---|---|---|
|  |  |  |
|  |  |  |
|  |  |  |
|  |  |  |
|  |  |  |
|  |  |  |

# LESSON *Plan*

| | |
|---|---|
| GROUP: | DATE: |
| BOOK TITLE: | LEVEL: |

## TEACHING POINT / STRATEGY

| WORD WORK | VOCABULARY |
|---|---|
| | |

## BEFORE READING

## DURING READING

## AFTER READING

## NOTES

# ANECDOTAL *Notes*

| STUDENT NAME | OBSERVATIONS | NOTES |
|---|---|---|
|  |  |  |
|  |  |  |
|  |  |  |
|  |  |  |
|  |  |  |
|  |  |  |

# LESSON *Plan*

GROUP:                                    DATE:

BOOK TITLE:                               LEVEL:

| TEACHING POINT / STRATEGY |
|---|

| WORD WORK | VOCABULARY |
|---|---|
|  |  |

## BEFORE READING

## DURING READING

## AFTER READING

## NOTES

# ANECDOTAL *Notes*

| STUDENT NAME | OBSERVATIONS | NOTES |
|---|---|---|
| | | |
| | | |
| | | |
| | | |
| | | |
| | | |

# LESSON *Plan*

GROUP:                                          DATE:

BOOK TITLE:                                      LEVEL:

## TEACHING POINT / STRATEGY

| WORD WORK | VOCABULARY |
|---|---|
|  |  |

## BEFORE READING

## DURING READING

## AFTER READING

## NOTES

# ANECDOTAL *Notes*

| STUDENT NAME | OBSERVATIONS | NOTES |
| --- | --- | --- |
|  |  |  |
|  |  |  |
|  |  |  |
|  |  |  |
|  |  |  |
|  |  |  |

# LESSON *Plan*

| GROUP: | DATE: |
|---|---|
| BOOK TITLE: | LEVEL: |

## TEACHING POINT / STRATEGY

| WORD WORK | VOCABULARY |
|---|---|
| | |

### BEFORE READING

### DURING READING

### AFTER READING

### NOTES

# ANECDOTAL *Notes*

| STUDENT NAME | OBSERVATIONS | NOTES |
|---|---|---|
|  |  |  |
|  |  |  |
|  |  |  |
|  |  |  |
|  |  |  |
|  |  |  |

# LESSON *Plan*

| | |
|---|---|
| GROUP: | DATE: |
| BOOK TITLE: | LEVEL: |

## TEACHING POINT / STRATEGY

| WORD WORK | VOCABULARY |
|---|---|
| | |

## BEFORE READING

## DURING READING

## AFTER READING

## NOTES

# ANECDOTAL Notes

| STUDENT NAME | OBSERVATIONS | NOTES |
|---|---|---|
|  |  |  |
|  |  |  |
|  |  |  |
|  |  |  |
|  |  |  |
|  |  |  |

# LESSON *Plan*

| GROUP: | DATE: |
|---|---|
| BOOK TITLE: | LEVEL: |

## TEACHING POINT / STRATEGY

| WORD WORK | VOCABULARY |
|---|---|
| | |

## BEFORE READING

## DURING READING

## AFTER READING

## NOTES

# ANECDOTAL *Notes*

| STUDENT NAME | OBSERVATIONS | NOTES |
|---|---|---|
|  |  |  |
|  |  |  |
|  |  |  |
|  |  |  |
|  |  |  |
|  |  |  |

# LESSON *Plan*

| GROUP: | DATE: |
|---|---|
| BOOK TITLE: | LEVEL: |

## TEACHING POINT / STRATEGY

| WORD WORK | VOCABULARY |
|---|---|
| | |

## BEFORE READING

## DURING READING

## AFTER READING

## NOTES

# ANECDOTAL Notes

| STUDENT NAME | OBSERVATIONS | NOTES |
|---|---|---|
|  |  |  |
|  |  |  |
|  |  |  |
|  |  |  |
|  |  |  |
|  |  |  |

# LESSON *Plan*

| | |
|---|---|
| GROUP: | DATE: |
| BOOK TITLE: | LEVEL: |

## TEACHING POINT / STRATEGY

| WORD WORK | VOCABULARY |
|---|---|
| | |

## BEFORE READING

## DURING READING

## AFTER READING

## NOTES

# ANECDOTAL *Notes*

| STUDENT NAME | OBSERVATIONS | NOTES |
|---|---|---|
|  |  |  |
|  |  |  |
|  |  |  |
|  |  |  |
|  |  |  |
|  |  |  |

# LESSON Plan

GROUP:                                           DATE:

BOOK TITLE:                              LEVEL:

| TEACHING POINT / STRATEGY |
| --- |
| |

| WORD WORK | VOCABULARY |
| --- | --- |
| | |

### BEFORE READING

### DURING READING

### AFTER READING

### NOTES

# ANECDOTAL Notes

| STUDENT NAME | OBSERVATIONS | NOTES |
|---|---|---|
|  |  |  |
|  |  |  |
|  |  |  |
|  |  |  |
|  |  |  |
|  |  |  |

# LESSON *Plan*

GROUP:                                    DATE:

BOOK TITLE:                               LEVEL:

| TEACHING POINT / STRATEGY |
|---|

| WORD WORK | VOCABULARY |
|---|---|
|  |  |

BEFORE READING

DURING READING

AFTER READING

NOTES

# ANECDOTAL *Notes*

| STUDENT NAME | OBSERVATIONS | NOTES |
| --- | --- | --- |
|  |  |  |
|  |  |  |
|  |  |  |
|  |  |  |
|  |  |  |
|  |  |  |

# LESSON *Plan*

| GROUP: | DATE: |
| --- | --- |
| BOOK TITLE: | LEVEL: |

## TEACHING POINT / STRATEGY

| WORD WORK | VOCABULARY |
| --- | --- |
| | |

## BEFORE READING

## DURING READING

## AFTER READING

## NOTES

# ANECDOTAL *Notes*

| STUDENT NAME | OBSERVATIONS | NOTES |
|---|---|---|
| | | |
| | | |
| | | |
| | | |
| | | |
| | | |

# LESSON *Plan*

| GROUP: | DATE: |
|--------|-------|
| BOOK TITLE: | LEVEL: |

## TEACHING POINT / STRATEGY

| WORD WORK | VOCABULARY |
|-----------|------------|
|           |            |

### BEFORE READING

### DURING READING

### AFTER READING

### NOTES

# ANECDOTAL *Notes*

| STUDENT NAME | OBSERVATIONS | NOTES |
| --- | --- | --- |
|  |  |  |
|  |  |  |
|  |  |  |
|  |  |  |
|  |  |  |
|  |  |  |

# LESSON *Plan*

| GROUP: | DATE: |
|--------|-------|
| BOOK TITLE: | LEVEL: |

## TEACHING POINT / STRATEGY

| WORD WORK | VOCABULARY |
|-----------|------------|
|           |            |

### BEFORE READING

### DURING READING

### AFTER READING

### NOTES

# ANECDOTAL *Notes*

| STUDENT NAME | OBSERVATIONS | NOTES |
|---|---|---|
| | | |
| | | |
| | | |
| | | |
| | | |
| | | |

# LESSON *Plan*

| GROUP: | DATE: |
|---|---|
| BOOK TITLE: | LEVEL: |

## TEACHING POINT / STRATEGY

| WORD WORK | VOCABULARY |
|---|---|
| | |

## BEFORE READING

## DURING READING

## AFTER READING

## NOTES

# ANECDOTAL *Notes*

| STUDENT NAME | OBSERVATIONS | NOTES |
|---|---|---|
|  |  |  |
|  |  |  |
|  |  |  |
|  |  |  |
|  |  |  |
|  |  |  |

# LESSON *Plan*

| GROUP: | DATE: |
|---|---|
| BOOK TITLE: | LEVEL: |

## TEACHING POINT / STRATEGY

| WORD WORK | VOCABULARY |
|---|---|
| | |

## BEFORE READING

## DURING READING

## AFTER READING

## NOTES

# ANECDOTAL Notes

| STUDENT NAME | OBSERVATIONS | NOTES |
|---|---|---|
|  |  |  |
|  |  |  |
|  |  |  |
|  |  |  |
|  |  |  |
|  |  |  |

# LESSON *Plan*

GROUP:                                         DATE:

BOOK TITLE:                             LEVEL:

## TEACHING POINT / STRATEGY

| WORD WORK | VOCABULARY |
|---|---|
|  |  |

## BEFORE READING

## DURING READING

## AFTER READING

## NOTES

# ANECDOTAL *Notes*

| STUDENT NAME | OBSERVATIONS | NOTES |
|---|---|---|
|  |  |  |
|  |  |  |
|  |  |  |
|  |  |  |
|  |  |  |
|  |  |  |

# LESSON Plan

GROUP:

DATE:

BOOK TITLE:

LEVEL:

| TEACHING POINT / STRATEGY |
|:-:|

| WORD WORK | VOCABULARY |
|:-:|:-:|

## BEFORE READING

## DURING READING

## AFTER READING

## NOTES

# ANECDOTAL *Notes*

| STUDENT NAME | OBSERVATIONS | NOTES |
|---|---|---|
|  |  |  |
|  |  |  |
|  |  |  |
|  |  |  |
|  |  |  |
|  |  |  |

# LESSON *Plan*

GROUP:                                    DATE:

BOOK TITLE:                               LEVEL:

## TEACHING POINT / STRATEGY

| WORD WORK | VOCABULARY |
| --- | --- |
|  |  |

## BEFORE READING

## DURING READING

## AFTER READING

## NOTES

# ANECDOTAL *Notes*

| STUDENT NAME | OBSERVATIONS | NOTES |
| --- | --- | --- |
| | | |
| | | |
| | | |
| | | |
| | | |
| | | |

# LESSON *Plan*

| GROUP: | DATE: |
|---|---|
| BOOK TITLE: | LEVEL: |

## TEACHING POINT / STRATEGY

| WORD WORK | VOCABULARY |
|---|---|
| | |

## BEFORE READING

## DURING READING

## AFTER READING

## NOTES

# ANECDOTAL *Notes*

| STUDENT NAME | OBSERVATIONS | NOTES |
|---|---|---|
|  |  |  |
|  |  |  |
|  |  |  |
|  |  |  |
|  |  |  |
|  |  |  |

# LESSON *Plan*

GROUP:

DATE:

BOOK TITLE:

LEVEL:

## TEACHING POINT / STRATEGY

| WORD WORK | VOCABULARY |
| --- | --- |
| | |

### BEFORE READING

### DURING READING

### AFTER READING

### NOTES

# ANECDOTAL Notes

| STUDENT NAME | OBSERVATIONS | NOTES |
|---|---|---|
| | | |
| | | |
| | | |
| | | |
| | | |
| | | |

# LESSON *Plan*

| GROUP: | DATE: |
| --- | --- |
| BOOK TITLE: | LEVEL: |

## TEACHING POINT / STRATEGY

| WORD WORK | VOCABULARY |
| --- | --- |
| | |

## BEFORE READING

## DURING READING

## AFTER READING

## NOTES

# ANECDOTAL *Notes*

| STUDENT NAME | OBSERVATIONS | NOTES |
| --- | --- | --- |
|  |  |  |
|  |  |  |
|  |  |  |
|  |  |  |
|  |  |  |
|  |  |  |

# LESSON *Plan*

GROUP: 

DATE: 

BOOK TITLE: 

LEVEL: 

## TEACHING POINT / STRATEGY

| WORD WORK | VOCABULARY |
|---|---|
|  |  |

—— BEFORE READING ——

—— DURING READING ——

—— AFTER READING ——

—— NOTES ——

# ANECDOTAL *Notes*

| STUDENT NAME | OBSERVATIONS | NOTES |
|---|---|---|
| | | |
| | | |
| | | |
| | | |
| | | |
| | | |

# LESSON *Plan*

GROUP:                                     DATE:

BOOK TITLE:                            LEVEL:

## TEACHING POINT / STRATEGY

| WORD WORK | VOCABULARY |
|---|---|
|  |  |

## BEFORE READING

## DURING READING

## AFTER READING

## NOTES

# ANECDOTAL *Notes*

| STUDENT NAME | OBSERVATIONS | NOTES |
|---|---|---|
| | | |
| | | |
| | | |
| | | |
| | | |
| | | |

# LESSON *Plan*

| | |
|---|---|
| GROUP: | DATE: |
| BOOK TITLE: | LEVEL: |

## TEACHING POINT / STRATEGY

| WORD WORK | VOCABULARY |
|---|---|
| | |

## BEFORE READING

## DURING READING

## AFTER READING

## NOTES

# ANECDOTAL *Notes*

| STUDENT NAME | OBSERVATIONS | NOTES |
|---|---|---|
|  |  |  |
|  |  |  |
|  |  |  |
|  |  |  |
|  |  |  |
|  |  |  |

# LESSON *Plan*

GROUP: DATE:

BOOK TITLE: LEVEL:

## TEACHING POINT / STRATEGY

| WORD WORK | VOCABULARY |
|---|---|
| | |

## BEFORE READING

## DURING READING

## AFTER READING

## NOTES

# ANECDOTAL *Notes*

| STUDENT NAME | OBSERVATIONS | NOTES |
|---|---|---|
|  |  |  |
|  |  |  |
|  |  |  |
|  |  |  |
|  |  |  |
|  |  |  |

# LESSON Plan

GROUP: 

DATE: 

BOOK TITLE: 

LEVEL: 

## TEACHING POINT / STRATEGY

| WORD WORK | VOCABULARY |
| --- | --- |
| | |

### BEFORE READING

### DURING READING

### AFTER READING

### NOTES

# ANECDOTAL Notes

| STUDENT NAME | OBSERVATIONS | NOTES |
|---|---|---|
|  |  |  |
|  |  |  |
|  |  |  |
|  |  |  |
|  |  |  |
|  |  |  |

# LESSON *Plan*

GROUP:                                  DATE:

BOOK TITLE:                      LEVEL:

## TEACHING POINT / STRATEGY

| WORD WORK | VOCABULARY |
|---|---|
|  |  |

## BEFORE READING

## DURING READING

## AFTER READING

## NOTES

# ANECDOTAL *Notes*

| STUDENT NAME | OBSERVATIONS | NOTES |
| --- | --- | --- |
|  |  |  |
|  |  |  |
|  |  |  |
|  |  |  |
|  |  |  |
|  |  |  |

# LESSON *Plan*

| GROUP: | DATE: |
|--------|-------|
| BOOK TITLE: | LEVEL: |

## TEACHING POINT / STRATEGY

| WORD WORK | VOCABULARY |
|-----------|------------|
|           |            |

## BEFORE READING

## DURING READING

## AFTER READING

## NOTES

# ANECDOTAL *Notes*

| STUDENT NAME | OBSERVATIONS | NOTES |
| --- | --- | --- |
| | | |
| | | |
| | | |
| | | |
| | | |
| | | |

# LESSON *Plan*

| GROUP: | DATE: |
|---|---|
| BOOK TITLE: | LEVEL: |

## TEACHING POINT / STRATEGY

| WORD WORK | VOCABULARY |
|---|---|
| | |

## BEFORE READING

## DURING READING

## AFTER READING

## NOTES

# ANECDOTAL *Notes*

| STUDENT NAME | OBSERVATIONS | NOTES |
|---|---|---|
|  |  |  |
|  |  |  |
|  |  |  |
|  |  |  |
|  |  |  |
|  |  |  |

# LESSON *Plan*

GROUP:                                          DATE:

BOOK TITLE:                                      LEVEL:

## TEACHING POINT / STRATEGY

| WORD WORK | VOCABULARY |
|---|---|
|  |  |

### BEFORE READING

### DURING READING

### AFTER READING

### NOTES

# ANECDOTAL Notes

| STUDENT NAME | OBSERVATIONS | NOTES |
|---|---|---|
|  |  |  |
|  |  |  |
|  |  |  |
|  |  |  |
|  |  |  |
|  |  |  |

# LESSON *Plan*

GROUP:                                          DATE:

BOOK TITLE:                                      LEVEL:

## TEACHING POINT / STRATEGY

| WORD WORK | VOCABULARY |
|---|---|
|  |  |

## BEFORE READING

## DURING READING

## AFTER READING

## NOTES

# ANECDOTAL *Notes*

| STUDENT NAME | OBSERVATIONS | NOTES |
|---|---|---|
|  |  |  |
|  |  |  |
|  |  |  |
|  |  |  |
|  |  |  |
|  |  |  |

# LESSON *Plan*

GROUP:                                              DATE:

BOOK TITLE:                                         LEVEL:

| TEACHING POINT / STRATEGY |
| --- |
|  |

| WORD WORK | VOCABULARY |
| --- | --- |
|  |  |

## BEFORE READING

## DURING READING

## AFTER READING

## NOTES

# ANECDOTAL *Notes*

| STUDENT NAME | OBSERVATIONS | NOTES |
|---|---|---|
|  |  |  |
|  |  |  |
|  |  |  |
|  |  |  |
|  |  |  |
|  |  |  |

# LESSON Plan

GROUP:                                    DATE:

BOOK TITLE:                               LEVEL:

| TEACHING POINT / STRATEGY |
|---|

| WORD WORK | VOCABULARY |
|---|---|

## BEFORE READING

## DURING READING

## AFTER READING

## NOTES

# ANECDOTAL *Notes*

| STUDENT NAME | OBSERVATIONS | NOTES |
|---|---|---|
|  |  |  |
|  |  |  |
|  |  |  |
|  |  |  |
|  |  |  |
|  |  |  |

# LESSON *Plan*

GROUP:

DATE:

BOOK TITLE:

LEVEL:

| TEACHING POINT / STRATEGY | |
|---|---|
| | |
| WORD WORK | VOCABULARY |
| | |

BEFORE READING

DURING READING

AFTER READING

NOTES

# ANECDOTAL *Notes*

| STUDENT NAME | OBSERVATIONS | NOTES |
|---|---|---|
|  |  |  |
|  |  |  |
|  |  |  |
|  |  |  |
|  |  |  |
|  |  |  |

# LESSON *Plan*

GROUP:                                      DATE:

BOOK TITLE:                                 LEVEL:

| TEACHING POINT / STRATEGY |
|---|

| WORD WORK | VOCABULARY |
|---|---|

## BEFORE READING

## DURING READING

## AFTER READING

## NOTES

# ANECDOTAL Notes

| STUDENT NAME | OBSERVATIONS | NOTES |
| --- | --- | --- |
| | | |
| | | |
| | | |
| | | |
| | | |
| | | |

# LESSON *Plan*

| GROUP: | DATE: |
|---|---|
| BOOK TITLE: | LEVEL: |

## TEACHING POINT / STRATEGY

| WORD WORK | VOCABULARY |
|---|---|
| | |

## BEFORE READING

## DURING READING

## AFTER READING

## NOTES

# ANECDOTAL *Notes*

| STUDENT NAME | OBSERVATIONS | NOTES |
|---|---|---|
| | | |
| | | |
| | | |
| | | |
| | | |
| | | |

# LESSON *Plan*

**GROUP:**                                          **DATE:**

**BOOK TITLE:**                                     **LEVEL:**

| TEACHING POINT / STRATEGY |
|---|

| WORD WORK | VOCABULARY |
|---|---|

## BEFORE READING

## DURING READING

## AFTER READING

## NOTES

# ANECDOTAL *Notes*

| STUDENT NAME | OBSERVATIONS | NOTES |
| --- | --- | --- |
|  |  |  |
|  |  |  |
|  |  |  |
|  |  |  |
|  |  |  |
|  |  |  |

# LESSON *Plan*

GROUP:                                          DATE:

BOOK TITLE:                                      LEVEL:

| TEACHING POINT / STRATEGY |
|---|

| WORD WORK | VOCABULARY |
|---|---|

BEFORE READING

DURING READING

AFTER READING

NOTES

# ANECDOTAL *Notes*

| STUDENT NAME | OBSERVATIONS | NOTES |
|---|---|---|
|  |  |  |
|  |  |  |
|  |  |  |
|  |  |  |
|  |  |  |
|  |  |  |

# LESSON *Plan*

| GROUP: | DATE: |
|---|---|
| BOOK TITLE: | LEVEL: |

## TEACHING POINT / STRATEGY

| WORD WORK | VOCABULARY |
|---|---|
|  |  |

### BEFORE READING

### DURING READING

### AFTER READING

### NOTES

# ANECDOTAL *Notes*

| STUDENT NAME | OBSERVATIONS | NOTES |
|---|---|---|
|  |  |  |
|  |  |  |
|  |  |  |
|  |  |  |
|  |  |  |
|  |  |  |

# LESSON *Plan*

GROUP:                                        DATE:

BOOK TITLE:                                   LEVEL:

| TEACHING POINT / STRATEGY |
|---|

| WORD WORK | VOCABULARY |
|---|---|
|  |  |

## BEFORE READING

## DURING READING

## AFTER READING

## NOTES

# ANECDOTAL Notes

| STUDENT NAME | OBSERVATIONS | NOTES |
|---|---|---|
| | | |
| | | |
| | | |
| | | |
| | | |
| | | |

# LESSON *Plan*

| GROUP: | DATE: |
|--------|-------|
| BOOK TITLE: | LEVEL: |

## TEACHING POINT / STRATEGY

| WORD WORK | VOCABULARY |
|-----------|------------|
|           |            |

## BEFORE READING

## DURING READING

## AFTER READING

## NOTES

# ANECDOTAL *Notes*

| STUDENT NAME | OBSERVATIONS | NOTES |
|---|---|---|
|  |  |  |
|  |  |  |
|  |  |  |
|  |  |  |
|  |  |  |
|  |  |  |

# LESSON *Plan*

GROUP:                                  DATE:

BOOK TITLE:                       LEVEL:

## TEACHING POINT / STRATEGY

| WORD WORK | VOCABULARY |
| --- | --- |
| | |

## BEFORE READING

## DURING READING

## AFTER READING

## NOTES

# ANECDOTAL *Notes*

| STUDENT NAME | OBSERVATIONS | NOTES |
|---|---|---|
|  |  |  |
|  |  |  |
|  |  |  |
|  |  |  |
|  |  |  |
|  |  |  |

# LESSON *Plan*

GROUP:                                                    DATE:

BOOK TITLE:                                               LEVEL:

| TEACHING POINT / STRATEGY |
|---|
| |

| WORD WORK | VOCABULARY |
|---|---|
| | |

## BEFORE READING

## DURING READING

## AFTER READING

## NOTES

# ANECDOTAL Notes

| STUDENT NAME | OBSERVATIONS | NOTES |
|---|---|---|
|  |  |  |
|  |  |  |
|  |  |  |
|  |  |  |
|  |  |  |
|  |  |  |

# LESSON _Plan_

GROUP:                                          DATE:

BOOK TITLE:                                      LEVEL:

## TEACHING POINT / STRATEGY

| WORD WORK | VOCABULARY |
| --- | --- |
|  |  |

## BEFORE READING

## DURING READING

## AFTER READING

## NOTES

# ANECDOTAL *Notes*

| STUDENT NAME | OBSERVATIONS | NOTES |
| --- | --- | --- |
|  |  |  |
|  |  |  |
|  |  |  |
|  |  |  |
|  |  |  |
|  |  |  |

# LESSON *Plan*

GROUP:                                          DATE:

BOOK TITLE:                                      LEVEL:

| TEACHING POINT / STRATEGY |
|---|

| WORD WORK | VOCABULARY |
|---|---|
|  |  |

## BEFORE READING

## DURING READING

## AFTER READING

## NOTES

# ANECDOTAL *Notes*

| STUDENT NAME | OBSERVATIONS | NOTES |
|---|---|---|
|  |  |  |
|  |  |  |
|  |  |  |
|  |  |  |
|  |  |  |
|  |  |  |

# Thank you!

For enquiries and feedback, please email us:

**365teacherresources@gmail.com**